MY SERMON NOTES

Date:
Pastor:
Church:

Book:
Verse:

SERMON NOTES

What does this passage teach me about God?

♪ SONGS ♪

CIRCLE THE WORDS YOU HEAR

Forgiveness
Salvation   Grace
Repent   Sin   Pray
Holy Spirit   Worship
Gospel   Jesus
Bible   Heaven
Love

MY SERMON NOTES

Date:
Pastor:
Church:

Book:
Verse:

SERMON NOTES

What does this passage teach me about God?

♫ SONGS ♫

Circle the words you hear

Forgiveness
Salvation   Grace
Repent   Sin   Pray
Holy Spirit   Worship
Gospel   Jesus
Bible   Heaven
Love

MY SERMON NOTES

Date:
Pastor:
Church:

Book:
Verse:

SERMON NOTES

What does this passage teach me about God?

♪ SONGS ♪

CIRCLE THE WORDS YOU HEAR

Forgiveness
Salvation   Grace
Repent   Sin   Pray
Holy Spirit   Worship
Gospel   Jesus
Bible   Heaven
Love

MY SERMON NOTES

Date:
Pastor:
Church:

Book:
Verse:

SERMON NOTES

What does this passage teach me about God?

🎵 SONGS 🎵

Circle the words you hear

Forgiveness
Salvation   Grace
Repent   Sin   Pray
Holy Spirit   Worship
Gospel   Jesus
Bible   Heaven
Love

MY SERMON NOTES

Date:
Pastor:
Church:

Book:
Verse:

SERMON NOTES

♪ SONGS ♪

What does this passage teach me about God?

Circle the words you hear

Forgiveness
Salvation   Grace
Repent   Sin   Pray
Holy Spirit   Worship
Gospel   Jesus
Bible   Heaven
Love

MY SERMON NOTES

Date:
Pastor:
Church:

Book:
Verse:

SERMON NOTES

What does this passage teach me about God?

🎵 SONGS 🎵

Circle the words you hear

Forgiveness
Salvation   Grace
Repent   Sin   Pray
Holy Spirit   Worship
Gospel   Jesus
Bible   Heaven
Love

MY SERMON NOTES

Date:
Pastor:
Church:

Book:
Verse:

SERMON NOTES

What does this passage teach me about God?

SONGS

Circle the words you hear

- Forgiveness
- Salvation   Grace
- Repent   Sin   Pray
- Holy Spirit   Worship
- Gospel   Jesus
- Bible   Heaven
- Love

MY SERMON NOTES

Date:
Pastor:
Church:

Book:
Verse:

SERMON NOTES

What does this passage teach me about God?

♪ SONGS ♪

CIRCLE THE WORDS YOU HEAR

Forgiveness
Salvation   Grace
Repent   Sin   Pray
Holy Spirit   Worship
Gospel   Jesus
Bible   Heaven
Love

MY SERMON NOTES

Date:
Pastor:
Church:

Book:
Verse:

SERMON NOTES

What does this passage teach me about God?

♪ SONGS ♪

Circle the words you hear

Forgiveness
Salvation   Grace
Repent   Sin   Pray
Holy Spirit   Worship
Gospel   Jesus
Bible   Heaven
Love

MY SERMON NOTES

Date:
Pastor:
Church:

Book:
Verse:

SERMON NOTES

What does this passage teach me about God?

♫ SONGS ♫

Circle the words you hear

- Forgiveness
- Salvation Grace
- Repent Sin Pray
- Holy Spirit Worship
- Gospel Jesus
- Bible Heaven
- Love

MY SERMON NOTES

Date:
Pastor:
Church:

Book:
Verse:

SERMON NOTES

What does this passage teach me about God?

♪ SONGS ♪

Circle the words you hear

Forgiveness
Salvation   Grace
Repent   Sin   Pray
Holy Spirit   Worship
Gospel   Jesus
Bible   Heaven
Love

MY SERMON NOTES

Date:
Pastor:
Church:

Book:
Verse:

SERMON NOTES

What does this passage teach me about God?

🎵 SONGS 🎵

Circle the words you hear

Forgiveness
Salvation   Grace
Repent   Sin   Pray
Holy Spirit   Worship
Gospel   Jesus
Bible   Heaven
Love

MY SERMON NOTES

Date:
Pastor:
Church:

Book:
Verse:

SERMON NOTES

What does this passage teach me about God?

♪ SONGS ♪

Circle the words you hear

Forgiveness
Salvation   Grace
Repent   Sin   Pray
Holy Spirit   Worship
Gospel   Jesus
Bible   Heaven
Love

MY SERMON NOTES

Date:
Pastor:
Church:

Book:
Verse:

SERMON NOTES

What does this passage teach me about God?

♪ SONGS ♪

Circle the words you hear

- Forgiveness
- Salvation   Grace
- Repent   Sin   Pray
- Holy Spirit   Worship
- Gospel   Jesus
- Bible   Heaven
- Love

MY SERMON NOTES

Date:
Pastor:
Church:

Book:
Verse:

SERMON NOTES

What does this passage teach me about God?

♫ SONGS ♫

Circle the words you hear

Forgiveness
Salvation   Grace
Repent   Sin   Pray
Holy Spirit   Worship
Gospel   Jesus
Bible   Heaven
Love

MY SERMON NOTES

Date:
Pastor:
Church:

Book:
Verse:

SERMON NOTES

What does this passage teach me about God?

♪ SONGS ♪

Circle the words you hear

Forgiveness
Salvation   Grace
Repent   Sin   Pray
Holy Spirit   Worship
Gospel   Jesus
Bible   Heaven
Love

MY SERMON NOTES

Date:
Pastor:
Church:

Book:
Verse:

SERMON NOTES

What does this passage teach me about God?

♫ SONGS ♫

Circle the words you hear

Forgiveness
Salvation   Grace
Repent   Sin   Pray
Holy Spirit   Worship
Gospel   Jesus
Bible   Heaven
Love

MY SERMON NOTES

Date:
Pastor:
Church:

Book:
Verse:

SERMON NOTES

What does this passage teach me about God?

♪ SONGS ♪

Circle the words you hear

Forgiveness
Salvation   Grace
Repent   Sin   Pray
Holy Spirit   Worship
Gospel   Jesus
Bible   Heaven
Love

MY SERMON NOTES

Date:
Pastor:
Church:

Book:
Verse:

SERMON NOTES

What does this passage teach me about God?

♫ SONGS ♫

Circle the words you hear

Forgiveness
Salvation   Grace
Repent   Sin   Pray
Holy Spirit   Worship
Gospel   Jesus
Bible   Heaven
Love

MY SERMON NOTES

Date:
Pastor:
Church:

Book:
Verse:

SERMON NOTES

What does this passage teach me about God?

♪ SONGS ♪

Circle the words you hear

Forgiveness
Salvation   Grace
Repent   Sin   Pray
Holy Spirit   Worship
Gospel   Jesus
Bible   Heaven
Love

MY SERMON NOTES

Date:
Pastor:
Church:

Book:
Verse:

SERMON NOTES

What does this passage teach me about God?

♪ SONGS ♪

Circle the words you hear

Forgiveness
Salvation   Grace
Repent   Sin   Pray
Holy Spirit   Worship
Gospel   Jesus
Bible   Heaven
Love

MY SERMON NOTES

Date:
Pastor:
Church:

Book:
Verse:

SERMON NOTES

What does this passage teach me about God?

♪ SONGS ♪

Circle the words you hear

- Forgiveness
- Salvation   Grace
- Repent   Sin   Pray
- Holy Spirit   Worship
- Gospel   Jesus
- Bible   Heaven
- Love

MY SERMON NOTES

Date:
Pastor:
Church:

Book:
Verse:

SERMON NOTES

What does this passage teach me about God?

♪ SONGS ♪

Circle the words you hear

Forgiveness
Salvation   Grace
Repent   Sin   Pray
Holy Spirit   Worship
Gospel   Jesus
Bible   Heaven
Love

MY SERMON NOTES

Date:
Pastor:
Church:

Book:
Verse:

SERMON NOTES

What does this passage teach me about God?

♪ SONGS ♪

Circle the words you hear

- Forgiveness
- Salvation
- Grace
- Repent
- Sin
- Pray
- Holy Spirit
- Worship
- Gospel
- Jesus
- Bible
- Heaven
- Love

MY SERMON NOTES

Date:
Pastor:
Church:

Book:
Verse:

SERMON NOTES

What does this passage teach me about God?

♪ SONGS ♪

Circle the words you hear

Forgiveness
Salvation   Grace
Repent   Sin   Pray
Holy Spirit   Worship
Gospel   Jesus
Bible   Heaven
Love

MY SERMON NOTES

Date:
Pastor:
Church:

Book:
Verse:

SERMON NOTES

What does this passage teach me about God?

♪ SONGS ♪

Circle the words you hear

- Forgiveness
- Salvation
- Grace
- Repent
- Sin
- Pray
- Holy Spirit
- Worship
- Gospel
- Jesus
- Bible
- Heaven
- Love

MY SERMON NOTES

Date:
Pastor:
Church:

Book:
Verse:

SERMON NOTES

What does this passage teach me about God?

♪ SONGS ♪

CIRCLE THE WORDS YOU HEAR

Forgiveness
Salvation   Grace
Repent   Sin   Pray
Holy Spirit   Worship
Gospel   Jesus
Bible   Heaven
Love

MY SERMON NOTES

Date:
Pastor:
Church:

Book:
Verse:

SERMON NOTES

What does this passage teach me about God?

♪ SONGS ♪

circle the words you hear

Forgiveness
Salvation   Grace
Repent   Sin   Pray
Holy Spirit   Worship
Gospel   Jesus
Bible   Heaven
Love

MY SERMON NOTES

Date:
Pastor:
Church:

Book:
Verse:

SERMON NOTES

What does this passage teach me about God?

♪ SONGS ♪

Circle the words you hear

Forgiveness
Salvation   Grace
Repent   Sin   Pray
Holy Spirit   Worship
Gospel   Jesus
Bible   Heaven
Love

MY SERMON NOTES

Date:
Pastor:
Church:

Book:
Verse:

SERMON NOTES

What does this passage teach me about God?

♪ SONGS ♪

Circle the words you hear

Forgiveness
Salvation   Grace
Repent   Sin   Pray
Holy Spirit   Worship
Gospel   Jesus
Bible   Heaven
Love

MY SERMON NOTES

Date:
Pastor:
Church:

Book:
Verse:

SERMON NOTES

What does this passage teach me about God?

♪ SONGS ♪

Circle the words you hear

Forgiveness
Salvation Grace
Repent Sin Pray
Holy Spirit Worship
Gospel Jesus
Bible Heaven
Love

MY SERMON NOTES

Date:
Pastor:
Church:

Book:
Verse:

SERMON NOTES

What does this passage teach me about God?

♪ SONGS ♪

CIRCLE THE WORDS YOU HEAR

Forgiveness
Salvation   Grace
Repent   Sin   Pray
Holy Spirit   Worship
Gospel   Jesus
Bible   Heaven
Love

MY SERMON NOTES

Date:
Pastor:
Church:

Book:
Verse:

SERMON NOTES

What does this passage teach me about God?

♫ SONGS ♫

Circle the words you hear

Forgiveness
Salvation Grace
Repent Sin Pray
Holy Spirit Worship
Gospel Jesus
Bible Heaven
Love

MY SERMON NOTES

Date:
Pastor:
Church:

Book:
Verse:

SERMON NOTES

What does this passage teach me about God?

♪ SONGS ♪

Circle the words you hear

Forgiveness
Salvation   Grace
Repent   Sin   Pray
Holy Spirit   Worship
Gospel   Jesus
Bible   Heaven
Love

MY SERMON NOTES

Date:
Pastor:
Church:

Book:
Verse:

SERMON NOTES

What does this passage teach me about God?

🎵 SONGS 🎵

Circle the words you hear

Forgiveness
Salvation   Grace
Repent   Sin   Pray
Holy Spirit   Worship
Gospel   Jesus
Bible   Heaven
Love

MY SERMON NOTES

Date:
Pastor:
Church:

Book:
Verse:

SERMON NOTES

What does this passage teach me about God?

♪ SONGS ♪

Circle the words you hear

Forgiveness
Salvation   Grace
Repent   Sin   Pray
Holy Spirit   Worship
Gospel   Jesus
Bible   Heaven
Love

MY SERMON NOTES

Date:
Pastor:
Church:

Book:
Verse:

SERMON NOTES

What does this passage teach me about God?

♫ SONGS ♫

CIRCLE THE WORDS YOU HEAR

Forgiveness
Salvation   Grace
Repent   Sin   Pray
Holy Spirit   Worship
Gospel   Jesus
Bible   Heaven
Love

MY SERMON NOTES

Date:
Pastor:
Church:

Book:
Verse:

SERMON NOTES

What does this passage teach me about God?

♪ SONGS ♪

Circle the words you hear

Forgiveness
Salvation   Grace
Repent   Sin   Pray
Holy Spirit   Worship
Gospel   Jesus
Bible   Heaven
Love

MY SERMON NOTES

Date:
Pastor:
Church:

Book:
Verse:

SERMON NOTES

What does this passage teach me about God?

♪ SONGS ♪

CIRCLE THE WORDS YOU HEAR

Forgiveness
Salvation   Grace
Repent   Sin   Pray
Holy Spirit   Worship
Gospel   Jesus
Bible   Heaven
Love

MY SERMON NOTES

Date:
Pastor:
Church:

Book:
Verse:

SERMON NOTES

What does this passage teach me about God?

♪ SONGS ♪

Circle the words you hear

- Forgiveness
- Salvation
- Grace
- Repent
- Sin
- Pray
- Holy Spirit
- Worship
- Gospel
- Jesus
- Bible
- Heaven
- Love

MY SERMON NOTES

Date:
Pastor:
Church:

Book:
Verse:

SERMON NOTES

What does this passage teach me about God?

♪ SONGS ♪

Circle the words you hear

Forgiveness
Salvation   Grace
Repent   Sin   Pray
Holy Spirit   Worship
Gospel   Jesus
Bible   Heaven
Love

MY SERMON NOTES

Date:
Pastor:
Church:
Book:
Verse:

SERMON NOTES

What does this passage teach me about God?

♫ SONGS ♫

Circle the words you hear

- Forgiveness
- Salvation
- Grace
- Repent
- Sin
- Pray
- Holy Spirit
- Worship
- Gospel
- Jesus
- Bible
- Heaven
- Love

MY SERMON NOTES

• •

Date:

Pastor:

Church:

Book:

Verse:

SERMON NOTES

What does this passage teach me about God?

♪ SONGS ♪

Circle the words you hear

Forgiveness
Salvation   Grace
Repent   Sin   Pray
Holy Spirit   Worship
Gospel   Jesus
Bible   Heaven
Love

MY SERMON NOTES

Date:
Pastor:
Church:

Book:
Verse:

SERMON NOTES

What does this passage teach me about God?

🎵 SONGS 🎵

Circle the words you hear

Forgiveness
Salvation   Grace
Repent   Sin   Pray
Holy Spirit   Worship
Gospel   Jesus
Bible   Heaven
Love

MY SERMON NOTES

Date:
Pastor:
Church:

Book:
Verse:

SERMON NOTES

What does this passage teach me about God?

♪ SONGS ♪

Circle the words you hear

Forgiveness
Salvation Grace
Repent Sin Pray
Holy Spirit Worship
Gospel Jesus
Bible Heaven
Love

MY SERMON NOTES

Date:
Pastor:
Church:

Book:
Verse:

SERMON NOTES

What does this passage teach me about God?

♪ SONGS ♪

Circle the words you hear

- Forgiveness
- Salvation
- Grace
- Repent
- Sin
- Pray
- Holy Spirit
- Worship
- Gospel
- Jesus
- Bible
- Heaven
- Love

MY SERMON NOTES

Date:
Pastor:
Church:

Book:
Verse:

SERMON NOTES

What does this passage teach me about God?

SONGS

Circle the Words You Hear

Forgiveness
Salvation Grace
Repent Sin Pray
Holy Spirit Worship
Gospel Jesus
Bible Heaven
Love

MY SERMON NOTES

Date:
Pastor:
Church:
Book:
Verse:

SERMON NOTES

♪ SONGS ♪

Circle the words you hear

Forgiveness
Salvation   Grace
Repent   Sin   Pray
Holy Spirit   Worship
Gospel   Jesus
Bible   Heaven
Love

What does this passage teach me about God?

MY SERMON NOTES

Date:
Pastor:
Church:

Book:
Verse:

SERMON NOTES

What does this passage teach me about God?

♪ SONGS ♪

Circle the words you hear

Forgiveness
Salvation   Grace
Repent   Sin   Pray
Holy Spirit   Worship
Gospel   Jesus
Bible   Heaven
Love

MY SERMON NOTES

Date:
Pastor:
Church:

Book:
Verse:

SERMON NOTES

What does this passage teach me about God?

♪ SONGS ♪

Circle the words you hear

- Forgiveness
- Salvation   Grace
- Repent   Sin   Pray
- Holy Spirit   Worship
- Gospel   Jesus
- Bible   Heaven
- Love

MY SERMON NOTES

Date:
Pastor:
Church:

Book:
Verse:

SERMON NOTES

What does this passage teach me about God?

♫ SONGS ♫

Circle the words you hear

Forgiveness
Salvation   Grace
Repent   Sin   Pray
Holy Spirit   Worship
Gospel   Jesus
Bible   Heaven
Love

MY SERMON NOTES

Date:
Pastor:
Church:
Book:
Verse:

SERMON NOTES

What does this passage teach me about God?

♪ SONGS ♪

Circle the words you hear

Forgiveness
Salvation Grace
Repent Sin Pray
Holy Spirit Worship
Gospel Jesus
Bible Heaven
Love

MY SERMON NOTES

Date:
Pastor:
Church:

Book:
Verse:

SERMON NOTES

What does this passage teach me about God?

♫ SONGS ♫

Circle the words you hear

Forgiveness
Salvation   Grace
Repent   Sin   Pray
Holy Spirit   Worship
Gospel   Jesus
Bible   Heaven
Love

MY SERMON NOTES

Date:
Pastor:
Church:

Book:
Verse:

SERMON NOTES

What does this passage teach me about God?

 SONGS

Circle the words you hear

- Forgiveness
- Salvation   Grace
- Repent   Sin   Pray
- Holy Spirit   Worship
- Gospel   Jesus
- Bible   Heaven
- Love

MY SERMON NOTES

Date:
Pastor:
Church:

Book:
Verse:

SERMON NOTES

What does this passage teach me about God?

♪ SONGS ♪

Circle the words you hear

- Forgiveness
- Salvation
- Grace
- Repent
- Sin
- Pray
- Holy Spirit
- Worship
- Gospel
- Jesus
- Bible
- Heaven
- Love

MY SERMON NOTES

Date:
Pastor:
Church:

Book:
Verse:

SERMON NOTES

What does this passage teach me about God?

♪ SONGS ♪

Circle the words you hear

Forgiveness
Salvation   Grace
Repent   Sin   Pray
Holy Spirit   Worship
Gospel   Jesus
Bible   Heaven
Love

MY SERMON NOTES

Date:
Pastor:
Church:

Book:
Verse:

SERMON NOTES

What does this passage teach me about God?

♪ SONGS ♪

Circle the words you hear

Forgiveness
Salvation   Grace
Repent   Sin   Pray
Holy Spirit   Worship
Gospel   Jesus
Bible   Heaven
Love

MY SERMON NOTES

Date:
Pastor:
Church:

Book:
Verse:

SERMON NOTES

What does this passage teach me about God?

♪ SONGS ♪

Circle the words you hear

Forgiveness
Salvation   Grace
Repent   Sin   Pray
Holy Spirit   Worship
Gospel   Jesus
Bible   Heaven
Love

MY SERMON NOTES

Date:
Pastor:
Church:

Book:
Verse:

SERMON NOTES

What does this passage teach me about God?

CIRCLE THE WORDS YOU HEAR

Forgiveness
Salvation   Grace
Repent   Sin   Pray
Holy Spirit   Worship
Gospel   Jesus
Bible   Heaven
Love

MY SERMON NOTES

Date:
Pastor:
Church:

Book:
Verse:

SERMON NOTES

What does this passage teach me about God?

♪ SONGS ♪

Circle the words you hear

- Forgiveness
- Salvation Grace
- Repent Sin Pray
- Holy Spirit Worship
- Gospel Jesus
- Bible Heaven
- Love

MY SERMON NOTES

Date:
Pastor:
Church:

Book:
Verse:

SERMON NOTES

What does this passage teach me about God?

🎵 SONGS 🎵

Circle the words you hear

Forgiveness
Salvation   Grace
Repent   Sin   Pray
Holy Spirit   Worship
Gospel   Jesus
Bible   Heaven
Love

MY SERMON NOTES

Date:
Pastor:
Church:

Book:
Verse:

SERMON NOTES

What does this passage teach me about God?

♫ SONGS ♫

Circle the words you hear

- Forgiveness
- Salvation
- Grace
- Repent
- Sin
- Pray
- Holy Spirit
- Worship
- Gospel
- Jesus
- Bible
- Heaven
- Love

MY SERMON NOTES

Date:
Pastor:
Church:

Book:
Verse:

SERMON NOTES

What does this passage teach me about God?

🎵 SONGS 🎵

Circle the words you hear

Forgiveness
Salvation   Grace
Repent   Sin   Pray
Holy Spirit   Worship
Gospel   Jesus
Bible   Heaven
Love

MY SERMON NOTES

Date:
Pastor:
Church:

Book:
Verse:

SERMON NOTES

What does this passage teach me about God?

♪ SONGS ♪

Circle the words you hear

Forgiveness
Salvation   Grace
Repent   Sin   Pray
Holy Spirit   Worship
Gospel   Jesus
Bible   Heaven
Love

MY SERMON NOTES

Date:
Pastor:
Church:

Book:
Verse:

SERMON NOTES

What does this passage teach me about God?

♪ SONGS ♪

CIRCLE THE WORDS YOU HEAR

Forgiveness
Salvation   Grace
Repent   Sin   Pray
Holy Spirit   Worship
Gospel   Jesus
Bible   Heaven
Love

MY SERMON NOTES

Date:
Pastor:
Church:

Book:
Verse:

SERMON NOTES

What does this passage teach me about God?

♪ SONGS ♪

Circle the words you hear

Forgiveness
Salvation   Grace
Repent   Sin   Pray
Holy Spirit   Worship
Gospel   Jesus
Bible   Heaven
Love

MY SERMON NOTES

Date:
Pastor:
Church:

Book:
Verse:

SERMON NOTES

What does this passage teach me about God?

SONGS

CIRCLE THE WORDS YOU HEAR

Forgiveness
Salvation   Grace
Repent   Sin   Pray
Holy Spirit   Worship
Gospel   Jesus
Bible   Heaven
Love

MY SERMON NOTES

Date:
Pastor:
Church:

Book:
Verse:

SERMON NOTES

What does this passage teach me about God?

♪ SONGS ♪

Circle the words you hear

Forgiveness
Salvation   Grace
Repent   Sin   Pray
Holy Spirit   Worship
Gospel   Jesus
Bible   Heaven
Love

MY SERMON NOTES

Date:
Pastor:
Church:

Book:
Verse:

SERMON NOTES

What does this passage teach me about God?

♪ SONGS ♪

Circle the words you hear

Forgiveness
Salvation Grace
Repent Sin Pray
Holy Spirit Worship
Gospel Jesus
Bible Heaven
Love

MY SERMON NOTES

Date:
Pastor:
Church:

Book:
Verse:

SERMON NOTES

What does this passage teach me about God?

♪ SONGS ♪

Circle the words you hear

Forgiveness
Salvation   Grace
Repent   Sin   Pray
Holy Spirit   Worship
Gospel   Jesus
Bible   Heaven
Love

Made in the USA
Coppell, TX
30 December 2023